ZE FRANK

YOUNG ME, NOW ME

Identical
Photos
Different
Decades

Ulysses
Press

Published in the United States by
ULYSSES PRESS
P.O. Box 3440
Berkeley, CA 94703
www.ulyssespress.com

ISBN 978-1-56975-982-0
Library of Congress Control Number 2011926037

Acquisitions editor: Kelly Reed
Managing editor: Claire Chun
Developmental editors: Caety Klingman, Kourtney Jason
Copy editors: Barbara Schultz, Lauren Harrison
Design and layout: what!design @ whatweb.com
Production: Judith Metzener
Front cover photos: © Barbara Brown and Kelly J. Brown
Back cover photos (from top to bottom): © Laura Gervais; © Maryam
    Al-Mukhaini and © Michael Fred Joyce; © Anke Vieth and © Annalena
    Vieth; © Donna G. Quann; © David Murray and Geneva B. Murray
Interior photos: see page 150

Printed in the United States by Bang Printing

10 9 8 7 6 5 4 3 2 1

Contents

Introduction

I joined Twitter in March of 2008 and quickly found myself wanting to see the faces of the people with whom I was tweeting. So to get a photo exchange started, I posted a link to an old photo of me as a child and tweeted, "This is what I looked like when I was little. What did you look like?" Hundreds of people responded in minutes. One of them suggested that I re-stage my childhood photograph, which you can see on the last page of this book. That is how *Young Me Now Me* was born.

To imitate a photograph from long ago is a strange and wonderful task. Since I began taking submissions, people have gone to great lengths—rounding up family members and gathering them in the same spot in the old backyard, sewing clothing to match styles that no longer exist, even smearing themselves in ice cream or spaghetti sauce to imitate the explosive lunchtime of a happy baby. Impressive, but the wonder comes from something else. When I look at that old picture, I am aware that it is of me but it is also not of me. My form has changed so radically over the years. I have stretched, widened, wrinkled, puffed, and roughened…there is hardly anything left of the original. But I am me.

On the website I ask participants to focus on the simple things: the face, the position of a wrist, the curve of a smile. That is where the wonder is. That is where you find the thread that connects years ago to now. The body changes, but the expressions hold their proportions and angles across time. The most basic photographs are often the most stunning, the ones where similarity pops out from under wrinkles and streaks of gray. Endlessly browse-able and endlessly personal. I am deeply indebted to everyone who participated. Visit www.zefrank.com/youngmenowme to add your own!

—Ze Frank

Creator, www.zefrank.com/youngmenowme

Rocket Man

I'd wanted a Rocket. It was a three-wheeled tricycle in blue. I'd seen it in Hamley's toy store and asked for it for Christmas. Come Christmas, I got some building blocks. They were nice, but I think I must have made a fuss about not getting the Rocket. Sometime afterward, I remember coming home from school, and in the middle of the

garden was The Tractor. I can't imagine being satisfied with a tractor out of the box, but I know I grew to love it as it was my first vehicle. Forty years later, as an adult, you can see me pictured behind the one thing I wanted all along—a speedy racing trike!

—Chris Joyce

Norway's Baddest Cowboys

My dad and his twin brother have always had matching faces, but when they were eight years old, they also donned brand-new matching cowboy outfits for the celebration of a Norwegian national holiday. Although they lived in the countryside on the Norwegian coast, they felt like the coolest cowboys on the street as they posed with real plastic pistols.

Forty-two years later, on their fiftieth birthday, the brothers decided to re-create this proud moment in the exact same spot. Unfortunately, not only were fringed vests and chaps impossible to find, but the vests they ended up with had to be cut in the back to stretch across their broad shoulders.

— *Kim Hansen*

Table Manners

Being Italian, I get way into eating my food. This is a major theme in my life. There are even family videos of me falling asleep into mashed potatoes. When I was two, my mom took a picture of me eating spaghetti as I pondered some deep questions like, Why did my parents give me a bib when all my sauce was just going to end up on my face? Though my sippy cup days are over, some things never change. I'm still a messy eater, and my family still tells me I have no restraint when I'm enjoying good food. Though I don't normally slop sauce on my cheeks, the *Now Me* picture is more indicative of my adult eating habits than you might imagine.

—*Lindsey Quann*

Straight *Faced*

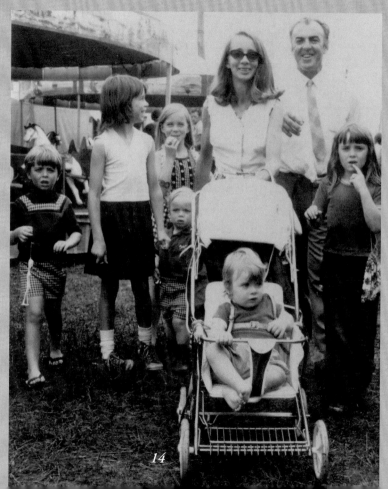

14

I n 1976, our family took a field trip to the local agricultural show in nearby Gulgong, Australia. We stood out from the crowd by being a crowd ourselves. We were even noticed by a photojournalist who captured the O'Brien clan on film and put us in the local newspaper. In 2010, with all of us reunited at the family farm for Christmas, we had big plans to restage the *Young Me* picture. Unfortunately the weather was not on our side; pouring rain forced us to move the photo shoot inside. Undaunted, we all got into position and tried our best to create the candid facial expressions we were wearing on that day twenty-four years ago.

— *Voren O'Brien*

Daddy's Little Monkey

These two pictures of me and George were taken forty-five years apart. My parents gave George to me on Thanksgiving in 1966. From that day forward, he was my constant companion and a family icon.

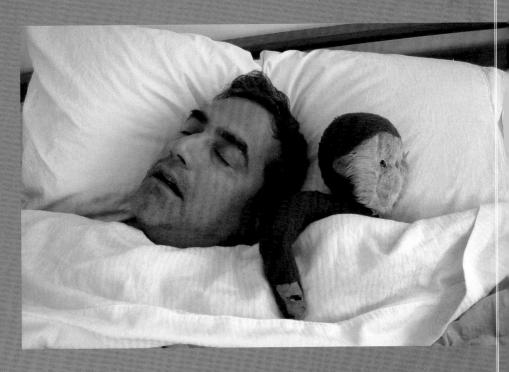

After I grew up and moved out, George came with me around the country from Boston to Austin to New York City. Though he no longer gets outside much or shares my bed with me (except for the taking of the *Now Me* photo), he does still hold court over my Manhattan apartment. A few months before my dad died, he gave me the *Young Me* picture from 1967. He called it "Bedtime for Steve and George."

— *Steven Dutton*

A Bridge to the Past

These pictures were taken in Hancock, Maryland, where my mother lived until the 1950s. In the original photo, taken around 1937, my mom was about eighteen years old. She is now ninety-two and suffers from Alzheimer's disease. She has lost most of her memories of the past, but amazingly, when I take her back to Hancock, she can describe living and working there decades ago, as if it were yesterday. She tells me about working as a waitress at the Park-n-Dine restaurant: "All the girls had to wear starched white uniforms and aprons." And she remembers selling peaches at a roadside stand: "People would come back year after year just to visit our peach stand."

— *Bill McKenney*

He Shoots, He Scores!

My son has adored sports since he was very young, particularly basketball. Even when he was too young to shoot on a regulation ten-foot-high rim, he loved practicing on his kiddie basket. Sometimes his grandfather would lift him up so that he could easily sink a bucket into his little five-foot hoop. My son is now sixteen years old and a towering six-foot-two high school varsity basketball player who can easily score on a real rim. Though my dad can no longer help him get air on the court, he still supports him by cheering him on. For the *Now Me* photo, Dad was tickled to imagine he was still able to lift his grandson flying into the air.

— *Steve Maller*

Little Worker Bee

When I was three years old, my grandmother made me a bee costume for a Carnival parade in Milan, Italy. She lovingly sewed wonderful costumes for my sister and me every year for Carnival, but I never won the prize for best costume. Now I work at the European Parliament in Brussels, where I re-created the *Young Me* photo. I rode the elevator to the available room, meeting a different colleague at each floor. They all stared at me as if I were a Martian! However, my very serious Spanish director laughed at me and said, "Well, the bees are said to be very hardworking!" These pictures are a tribute to my adored grandma, who didn't have a chance to meet the *Now Me*, but who would be very pleased to be mentioned.

— *Raffaella De Marte*

Mobile *Playhouse*

On a hot summer day in 1987, my kids were playing in the yard when something drove up to the house that instantly pulled them away from their games. It was a big, new station wagon their dad had just purchased. My kids were super excited about the new car—well, it was actually used, but it was new to them! They were very anxious for us to go on our next family road trip, when they could all ride in the back with lots of books and toys. So they piled inside, even though we weren't going anywhere. In 2010 I took the *Now Me* photo of them in the back of a large SUV, though apparently it wasn't large enough, because there's no longer room for their books, toys, or even my son's foot!

—*Barbara Brown*

Brotherly Love

If it looks like I'm not thrilled by the arrival of my newborn little brother, it's because I thought he was a screaming, pooping annoyance. As the years passed, and we got a bit older, we experienced the typical sibling rivalry. Luckily our Christmases together were saved by Santa, who apparently had figured out a way to prevent the brotherly arguing. He had an eye for presentation in our house: My stuff was on the right. Ben's on

the left. With a clear dividing line between the goods. So, this is what we awoke to on Christmas morning 1984: Snake Mountain for me. Castle Grayskull for him. Three He-Man vehicles for me. Three He-Man vehicles for him. Four He-Man action figures for me. Four for him. It blew. Our. F*&king. Little. Minds. Joy to the world, indeed!

— *Brantley Aufill*

Man at Work

M y grandfather has always been a do-it-yourself handyman. He's the go-to
artisan who can build stuff from scratch. In the *Young Me* photo taken back
in 1955, he was stationed at Parks Air Force Base and he was about to tackle an entire floor-refinishing project at the house he was living in near the base.

In more recent years, as he has gotten older, my grandfather has made some adjustments. He is more comfortable sitting than crouching and he uses smaller tools to complete smaller projects. The *Now Me* photo was taken in 2009 as we prepared to build a spice rack for the kitchen.

—*Phil Gorrindo*

Wild Things

The *Young Me* photo of my brother and me hung in the hallway of our home with other treasured family portraits. Because we were tow-heads and grew up in the fields and woods of New Hampshire, people called us *Children of the Corn*; it was a dubious reference, as my brother was clearly a bit of a clown and would often break down in helpless giggles over his own antics. In the twenty-five-plus years since the *Young Me* picture was taken, we've moved across the country in separate directions, married, and eventually made our separate ways back to New England, where we now live a few hours apart. We've remained close through the years, and being near the fields and woods again made it easy to re-create this photo.

— Courtney Collins

Quilted *Memories*

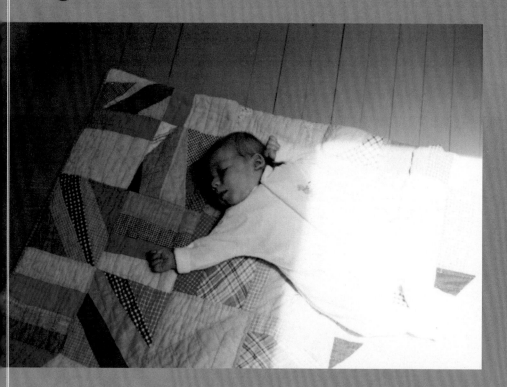

When my mom moved to the city, she gave my sister and me some of her old furniture. Mom packed everything very carefully because she didn't want anything to break, so the furniture came wrapped in old blankets and comforters. One lamp I received came bundled up in an antique quilt. I recognized the quilt right off from pictures of me when I was an infant. You can see that the fabric swatches match perfectly, though they've faded quite a bit. My sister showed both of these pictures to my mom, but she couldn't believe it. She said, "Wow, that almost looks like the exact same quilt. But he couldn't possibly have that!"

— *Ethan Wolff*

The Floating Girl

I did something a little out of the ordinary for my daughter Caitlin's senior photo. I made her a satin dress and took pictures of her wearing it as she floated in the pool like a mermaid. Among the many pictures I took was a close-up with her face partly out of the water. Shortly after her graduation, my other daughter, Kyla, was going through old photos and was stunned to find a picture I had taken of Caitlin floating in the bathtub with her cute baby face popping out of the water. I had long forgotten ever taking that picture, yet her senior photo looks just like it!

— *Lori Dill*

Thicker Than Water

My older brother, Jeff, was my best buddy when we were growing up, but we were very different as kids. I would quietly stick to my mother's side, whereas Jeff was independent, loud, and boisterous. But we still did almost everything together, including "painting the house." This was one of our mom's tricks to keep us occupied for a few hours; she'd send us out to the patio with brushes and a bucket of water. Despite the strains of our teen years, and our living in different cities for college, I still look up to my older brother. I have the deepest love and respect for Jeff, as he's always cared for me in a way no one else could, and he understands me effortlessly.

— *Teresa Murphy*

Everlasting Tradition

The *Young Me* photo with that special hat and necklace really shows how over-the-top my mother would make our birthday celebrations. But the best of all of my mom's birthday traditions was her ritual of making the birthday kid breakfast in bed. My birthday often fell on the first day of school, but she would still get up early and treat me like a princess. Now my sister carries on the tradition with each of her six kids. And once we each have kids, my brother and I plan to do the same.

— *Paige Russell*

School of
Thought

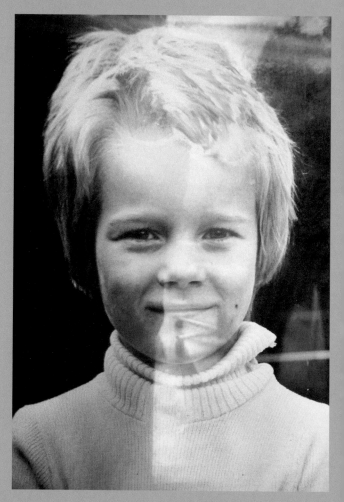

In the *Young Me* photo, I was six years old and living in the town of Kolding, Denmark. It was 1981, which was the first year I attended school. I took the *Now Me* picture at work as part of our annual Christmas party video in the European Parliament. I thought it was extremely funny to remake the original picture and try to get the facial expressions just right. Even though work at a very serious institution doing important work, I had fun last winter making the video and seeing how the picture turned out.

—*Olav Gade*

Parent Trap

When I was a child, my parents said I was "noisy" and "bold," and they would threaten to punish me if I didn't behave. Often, I would test these threats to see if my parents would actually follow through with them. They always did. But there was one threat that I didn't have the courage to test. On the day this picture was taken, my parents were trying to take a family photo in front of the fireplace. They told me that if I didn't behave like my brother and sister, I would get coal in my stocking for Christmas. As you can see from my face, that was a threat I didn't take lightly.

—Sue Remick

All in the Family

My extended family took a vacation to Fiji one year. My sister and I were able to meet our baby cousins and their parents on a remote island and really get to know them. We lived as locals for a couple of weeks—eating coconuts, swimming in the river, and snorkeling. Today, we all live far from each other in different countries, so plenty of long flights were needed to get us back together for another family reunion. After fifteen years, there was a lot of catching up to do! The little baby boy in the *Young Me* photo is not so little anymore and he was away picking fruit, so I substituted my own baby girl for the *Now Me* photo.

— *Mary Musthofa*

Friends till the End

Many of my childhood memories include Sandra. If you can't see her in the *Young Me* picture, it's probably because she was an imaginary friend and there is a very good chance she was with me as I rode my bike that day. It probably sounds weird, but it was nothing like the movie *Drop Dead Fred*.

One time, we were walking down the street in the middle of town and I was talking to Sandra loudly about something. I was probably just trying to entertain myself, but my mom did not like it. She shouted at me to stop! So I put Sandra in my pocket and told her quietly, "Shhhh…Mom is angry. We'll talk later."

—*Branka Malenica*

Daddy's Girl

In Soviet Latvia where I grew up, it wasn't common for people to own cameras. To take family photos, you'd pay for a photo shoot at a salon or borrow a camera. Either way, it was always a big production. The *Young Me* picture was arranged by my mom and nanny—but my father wasn't around. The *Now Me* picture was taken as part of my current employer's Christmas project called "Young us, Now us. The past always leaves a path…you can run, but you cannot hide." That is so true. Seeing these pictures together, I realize *I can run but cannot hide* from the fact that my father has always been slightly absent in my life.

— *Maija Krastina*

Life's a Beach!

When I was a kid, the typical family vacation for my mum, dad, me, and my twin brothers was a trip to Llanfairfechan in North Wales. There was not much there but the sea, sand, and beach, which pleased my dad as there was nothing much to spend money on! My own family doesn't vacation in Llanfairfechan, but we drive though there fairly often and I always insist on stopping even though my wife groans and rolls her eyes because there's nothing to see there. But I love it. Everything that was there when I was a kid is still there. I get to be eight again, walking on the beach and having a Horlicks and a custard pie at the pavilion.

— *Paul Whitehead*

Black and
White

My two kids, Katie and Michael, are nothing alike. Katie sprang from the womb talking. She could communicate even without words, and by the age of two, she was speaking in full sentences. Michael, on the other hand, was quiet, just like his dad. He was literally tongue-tied at birth, so the doctor had to snip below his tongue for him to eat properly. Whereas Katie loved words, Michael was drawn to numbers. When my husband helped Katie with her arithmetic, Michael chimed in with the answers. And if Michael and I played a memory game, he would always win, even when he was a toddler.

—*Mary Klein*

Hockey for Life

For us four kids living in Canada, our lives were all about hockey, hockey, hockey. We played on the road until it got dark, and then we would move inside and play in our basement. In the early 1970s, we even tried to make it into the *Guinness Book of World Records* for the longest game of ball hockey. We had heard the

record was ten hours, so we smashed it by playing from 7 a.m. to 7 p.m. My dad filmed it on his little Super 8 camera for proof. We later found out we were dozens of hours short of the actual record, but we did make it into the local community newspaper—and we thought that was about the coolest thing possible!

—*Jonathan Zweig*

Thrill of the Hunt

My dad's an avid hunter. Sometimes, when I was a little girl, I would go with him on a hunt and I would insist on wearing the appropriate attire: his camouflage gear. In reality, I was far too young to go hunting. My father was just taking me for walks in the woods, but the *Young Me* thought we were hunting. In the *Now Me* picture, I'm wearing my husband's coat and hat. Going from Dad's hunting gear to my husband's is really perfect. Turns out, back when we were dating, my now-husband asked my father's permission to marry me when the two of them were out hunting in Montana (and consequently heavily armed). A brave move in my opinion!

—*Julia Loeckner*

Some Things Never Change

Both of these pictures were taken in my living room in Rome. In the *Young Me* photo, I was 15 and a student in high school. The *Now Me* photo shows me sitting in the living room of the same apartment—the place I've called home since the day I was born.

Over the years, the apartment has stayed the same, as you can see. The chair and sofa look different, but that is only new material on the same frames. The rugs, pictures, lamp, and the decorative bird on the bookshelf haven't moved much, if at all, since that early picture was taken. And they'll probably stay in the same place for years to come.

—Alessio Maldini

Fish in Troubled Waters

When I was four, my grandfather took my two-year-old cousin and me on our first fishing trip. With plenty of help from Grandpa, I caught a perch and my cousin caught two. When Grandpa decided it was time to leave, I didn't think it was fair that I had only one fish but my cousin had two, so I threw quite a fit about it. Back at the house, my dad took the *Young Me* picture of me still looking really peeved and holding my *one* perch.

This past summer when I visited Grandpa's house, I decided to re-create the picture. I still haven't caught a second perch from the lake (that's a grocery store trout), but now I have a four-year-old girl myself, and I can totally appreciate what I put my grandpa and dad through.

—*Kitty Cakalan*

Sister, Sister

In the *Young Me* picture, my sister and I were photographed sharing a comic book when we were just five and eight. But, apparently, back then we didn't always get along as well as it looks in the photo. No one in our family remembers that specific moment in 1978, at our home in Orange, Connecticut, but the caption in the scrapbook says simply, "Sometimes friends—often rivals." Fortunately, the re-created photo, taken thirty-two years later in Costa Rica, does give an accurate portrait of our friendship today. Now we're always friends—never rivals!

—*Jennifer Tucker*

One Size Fits All

The *Young Me* photo was taken in 1981. It was during the Communist era in Poland when it was almost impossible to buy children's clothes in shops. My parents were able to acquire that fur coat because a friend had gone to Turkey and brought back coats to sell on the black market. Although the coat was two sizes too big, my parents were happy because I would be able to wear the coat for a number of years. But before I had a chance to grow into it, my aunt came to visit from the UK. My parents wanted to give her a nice picture of me, so they had me pose in my best clothes—my fancy new oversized black-market fur.

—*Karolina Woźniak*

Juiced Up

The *Young Me* picture of me and my brother was taken in 1994. Like most little kids, we drank our fair share of boxed juice. When my mother recently found that old photo, she mentioned that she still has some of those same juice boxes up in one of the kitchen cabinets.

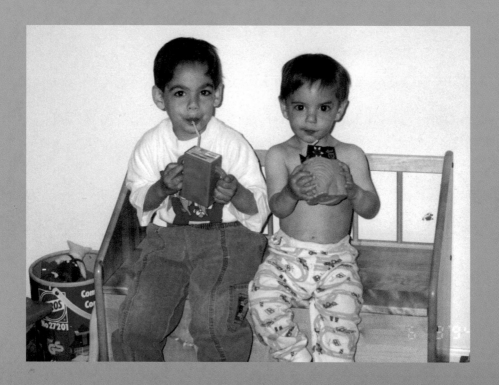

So the three of us decided to re-create the picture to celebrate fifteen years of fun with juice boxes! Watching this whole scene unfold, my father asked the question the rest hadn't thought to ask: "Why do we still have juice boxes with sippy straws around the house?"

—*Zach Schonfeld*

A Goal for Gran

My grandparents bought me my first soccer uniform. Little did I know that my Gran had nearly fainted when she saw the high price. But she had promised she would buy it for me, and she was a woman of her word. I loved the outfit so much that I wore it for a week straight. I felt so proud to be in that uniform, supporting my team, and I remembered that feeling well when I put on a jersey to pose for the *Now Me* picture.

—*Andrea Kate Miller*

Computer Whiz

From a very young age, I have always had a great interest in personal computers. I was thrilled when my family finally got one for our house. Back then, computers didn't have the sleekest and sexiest shape. The CPU looked like a flattened shoe box with a keyboard stuck on top, and the monitor could have passed for a cheap 1950s TV, but I spent hours on that family computer. And loved it.

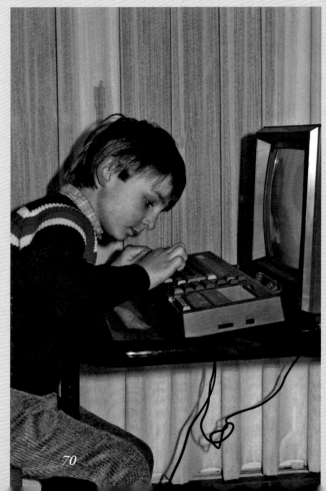

As I grew up and got bigger, computers got much, much smaller. However, twenty years later, I still spend hours on my computer every day—only now, it's usually in a more professional way.

—*Nicolas Wierzejewski*

Family Circus

The *Young Me* photo is of my little sister and me on our first overseas holiday to visit our grandparents in London. Our joy over having traveled for 30 hours by plane to a new country had to be expressed in some way, so naturally upon arrival we cracked out the face paint and dressed up as clowns. The funny thing is we used to fight like cats and dogs at that age, so neither of us can remember how we managed to get through an activity together, much less pose for this photo. Luckily, we get along a lot better these days. We recently coordinated a trip to our parents' house on the other side of Australia, so naturally upon arrival we cracked out the face paint and dressed up as clowns.

—*Kirsten Marks*

Belly Up

A fter seeing the motorcycle a friend had purchased, I immediately had déjà vu about a bike I was photographed with in my childhood. I searched and searched through old photos, and my flashback was right—the motorcycles were the same

model! I always thought it was such a funny picture of me as a little girl because I stuck out my tummy so far, so it was fitting that I was nine months pregnant for the *Now Me* re-creation since my tummy was sticking out without me even trying. A few days later, my own little girl was born, but I didn't name her Honda.

— *Kari Moyle*

Pillow Talk

Who can say why we all posed in such a ridiculous way for the *Young Me* photo? I think my brothers, Darius and Zachary, really wanted to look pregnant, so we

stuck pillows under our shirts. Fifteen years later for the *Now Me* picture, we managed to perfectly match our little kid outfits (luckily jeans, sweatpants, and brightly colored cotton shirts don't go out of style), although we did need much bigger and fluffier pillows to fully re-create that nine-months-along look. Our younger sibling, Sophia, didn't need any pillow to perfectly recapture her look of utter disdain at the whole scene.

—*Chloë Lind*

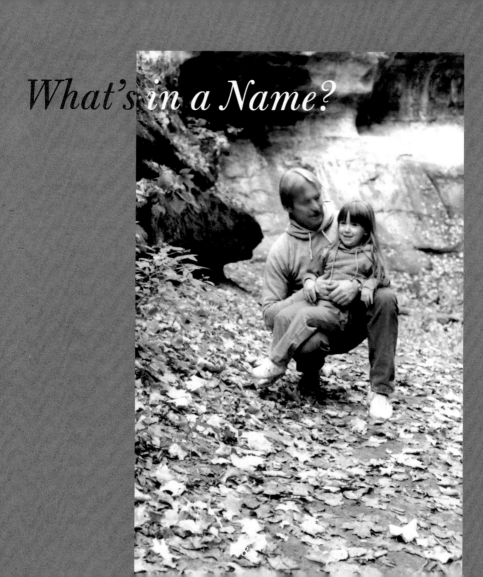

What's in a Name?

78

I don't remember the hike where we took that *Young Me* picture of my dad and me. But I do remember one time a couple of years later when I was about eight. We were riding in his truck and bonding over our favorite album, Harry Nilsson's *Nilsson Schmilssonn.* I asked my dad what his middle name was and he told me it was "Bingham." At first I thought he was lying so I said, "That's not a name, that's just a noise!" When he told me he was serious, I laughed so hard that I couldn't stop the entire way home. I guess my laughter hurt his feelings a little because he still brings it up eighteen years later. Sorry, Dad.

— Kim Craig

Number Cruncher

The *Young Me* picture of my dad was taken in 1955 when he was twenty-six-years old. How fitting that the camera was being wielded by his brother, who went on to become a professional photographer. Even more fitting is that the photo shows my dad doing what he has always loved—engineering. He tried to teach us kids how to use that darn slide rule, but it never made any sense to me.

81

The *Now Me* photo of Dad had to be staged since he has graduated to using modern calculators, but he still has that old slide rule and remembers exactly how to use it. My dad, the quintessential engineer.

——*Mimi Franklin Musso*

Time Flies

A couple of years ago, I posted the *Young Me* photo of "four-year-old Matt's first day of school" as my profile picture on Facebook. I left it there for more than a year. Meanwhile, I went about re-enacting it. I already owned the jeans, and I was able to find a pair of red suspenders easily enough. The shirt was harder; I had to have it custom-printed. Last, after much searching, I managed to find a similar-looking light blue lunch box on eBay. Then, on Halloween, I put it all together as my costume and surprised my friends with this re-created *Now Me* profile pic.

— *Matt Gervais*

Jingle Bells

As a special Christmas day outfit, I made my son Tague the *Young Me* "jingle suit" by sewing dozens of bells onto his little red onesie. Years later, I made an adult version of the same suit for grown-up Tague. And even though he only needed to wear it to take the *Now Me* picture, he wore his adult-sized onesie over his regular clothes all day on Christmas. It was great to see him embrace the silliness of the situation and show he hasn't lost his carefree, childlike attitude.

—*Jamie Hurley*

Play Ball

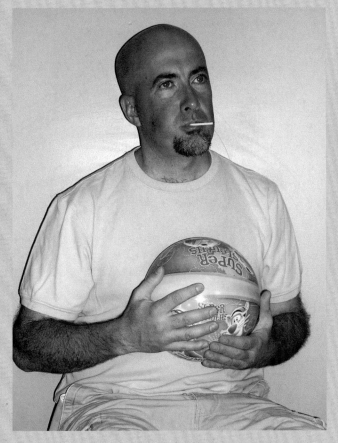

This *Young Me* photo, taken when I was 18 months old, is a perfect representation of my childhood. As a kid, I was nearly always seen with some kind of ball or some kind of lollipop. Even if it wasn't a baseball or football, as long as I had some kind of ball, I was the happiest kid around. And lollipops? I swear I made excuses to go to the doctor so I could get one. These days I tend to favor chocolate chip cookies, but I do still like my lollies, and though I'm now in my forties, there is still some kind of ball within my reach at all times.

—*John Mihaljevic*

Baby, *You're a Firework*

Both pictures of my wife, Savannah, and our son, Richie (he's hiding in the first shot), were taken on the Fourth of July, one year apart. In the *Young Me* picture, she was less than a week away from having our son. At the time, we were living in the Washington, D.C., metro area because I was in the Army and stationed in Virginia. The days when both of these pictures were taken were spent in the same way. We enjoyed the afternoon lounging by the kiddie pool at our apartment complex. Then in the evening, we headed to the National Mall to see the incredible fireworks display from the base of the Washington Monument.

— *Richie Rauscher*

A Rose Is a Rose Is a Rose

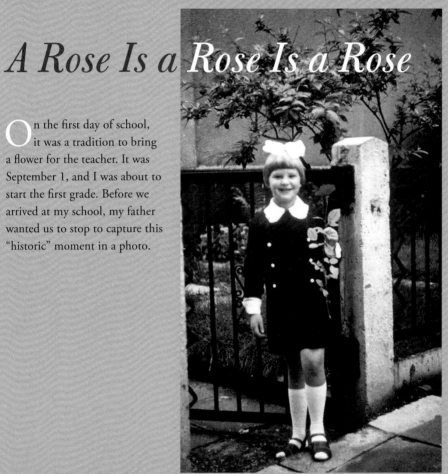

On the first day of school, it was a tradition to bring a flower for the teacher. It was September 1, and I was about to start the first grade. Before we arrived at my school, my father wanted us to stop to capture this "historic" moment in a photo.

Thirty years later, it felt strange, though lovely at the same time, to revisit my youth and recall what it felt like to hold a flower to be given to my teacher for the first time, and to be ready to meet new challenges in life that awaited me.

——*Asta Vasiliauskaite*

Playing the Field

My sister Ashleigh and I loved being outside when we were little kids. One of the funniest stories I can remember about us, though it's not from the hiking trip pictured in the *Young Me* photo, happened when we were on a little league softball team together. Back then, we didn't exactly know all the rules, and we were never sure if the left- and right-field positions related to the point of view of the fielders, or the batter. If one of us was assigned to the outfield, she would just wait until our teammates were in position, and then go to the opposite field. But one time our coach put me in left field and Ashleigh in right, and we didn't know what to do!

— *Lindsay Olix*

A Moment in Time

With lives spanning nearly a century, my mom and her two sisters are their own slice of American history. The *Young Me* picture of the Canaday girls—Beryl, Virginia, and Edith—was taken in 1922 and then re-created eight-nine years later. These three sisters have seen so many things: the Roaring 20s, the Great Depression, World War II—during which Beryl worked for the famous Fred Harvey Company at Kansas City's Union Station, and both Virginia and

Edith did their part for the war effort by working as Rosie the Riveters. After the war, these three remarkable women worked and raised families. Beryl retired at age eighty-two! Virginia was a nurse who married her patient, the love of her life. Edith played the violin in the Tulsa Symphony and is still an avid fisherwoman. They are all characters!

—*Geneva Murray*

Flower Power

I had just woken up when my father took this *Young Me* picture of me in my very 1970s orange flower wallpapered bedroom. I'm holding my brother's teddy bear and sitting in my older sister's bed, so I'm guessing I had just taken an afternoon nap. I have such great memories of that room my sister and I shared. We had so much fun playing there. And as we got older, we'd stay up until the early morning giggling and talking about everything. I succeeded in re-creating my happy look for the *Now Me* picture, but it is a lot harder as an adult to wake up and instantly be in such a good mood. Maybe some orange flower wallpaper would help.

—*Karin Friedrich Fromm*

Teddy Bear Hug

My bear Dieter was my favorite toy for years. My mom had to stitch him up several times because he was so worn out. Just look at the feet! But eventually I forgot about him. One day many years later, I looked through the closets at my parents' house to see what I would discover from my youth. I wasn't looking for Dieter, but I found him wrapped in a plastic bag, and I immediately shouted, "Dieter! Where have you been?!" It was pure joy. I felt like a little boy again. Now I'm taking the best care of him. He's sitting in my place, very well protected.

—Joerg Hoyer

Baby, You Can Drive My Car

Sitting by my side on the sofa in the *Young Me* photo is one of my toys from when I was a very young child—a model car. But that's not some generic toy car, it's a replica of the sporty little French car sold back in the late 1970s throughout Europe as the Renault 5 Alpine and in the United States as Le Car.

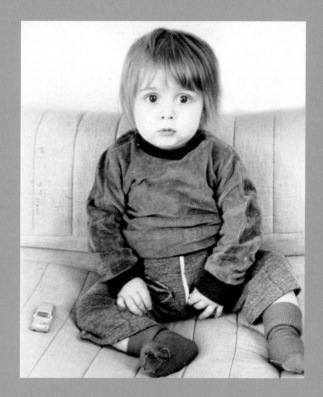

Thirty years later for the *Now Me* photo, I didn't have my old toy car available, so I replaced it with a toy version of a modern stylish and sporty little car—the Mini. As it turns out, my actual full-sized car is also a Mini.

—*Pierre Culot*

Sew What?

When I was very young, my god-mother, Verla, sewed the apron in the *Young Me* picture and embroidered the kitten and my name on it. Throughout my childhood, my grand-mother and her sisters provided my family with a steady supply of hand-made quilts and afghans. They weren't the only ones in the family who sewed, though. When my mom was in high school, she made most of her own clothes. She had learned

to sew from her mother, and eventually she taught me. My first sewing project was in seventh grade, when my mom helped me make a beautiful red Chinese-style dress for my school dance, using the old Singer sewing machine she's had since she was twelve.

—*Alexis Schad*

Tomato, Tomahto

These pictures of my cousin Randy and me were taken seventeen years apart. The garden in the background makes it look like they could be in the same yard, but they aren't. The *Young Me* photo was taken in our grandpa's backyard in Omaha, Nebraska, but the *Now Me* photo was taken in my dad's backyard thousands of miles away in California.

Even though their gardens are in different parts of the country, both my dad and grandpa were able to grow amazing tomatoes and giant zucchini that were more than a foot long and four inches in diameter. As long as I can remember, my family has always grown our own vegetables, and the two of them really have quite the green thumbs.

—*Jennifer Kelpe*

Playing Politics

My father George is an Egyptian-born Canadian who has long wished that we lived in a united North America. You can see how proudly he displays the flags of the U.S. and Canada. The stack of political and computer books by his side in both pictures makes it clear that his interests haven't changed. He's also remained attached to his "son" (and thus my "brother") Timmy Bird from 1986, when Timmy and I were two years old, to 2011. The one thing that has changed is the technology he uses. Back then, he had a Corona personal computer. Thankfully, he now works on an Apple laptop—a nice change.

—Janet Cordahi

Music Models

Carol and I first met at music camp on the Florida State University campus in 1977. It was the first of three occasions we spent there together as high schoolers. Then in 1980 when we both enrolled at FSU, we got to room together. The *Young Me* picture is of us as eighteen-year-old freshmen in the FSU music dorm.

Time passed and although we tried to stay in touch, our last visit was in 1986. Then 30 years after our first meeting, we reconnected via Facebook, and in 2009 Carol came for a visit. Coincidently, my husband had recently moved his old upright piano from storage into our house. With all the pieces in place, we decided to re-create the original pic.

——*Karen Beth Sweat*

Every Rose Has Its Thorn

The *Young Me* photo was taken at the Park of Roses in Columbus, Ohio. The rose park is just one section of the larger Whetstone Park, where we used to go all the time when I was a kid to pick berries, roll down the hills, and, well, smell the roses, of course. The *Now Me* photo was taken in a different rose park that's over a thousand miles away from Columbus but in none other than the City of Roses, Portland, Oregon. As to what I was doing in the *Young Me* photo? Probably stealing a rose, riffraff that I was.

—*Mime Čuvalo*

Worth a

he *Young Me* picture from 1984 is a favorite image in our family and has always hung on one wall or another in our parents' house.

Re-creating the picture took a bit of effort. We had to get all the clothes and props
right—that's the same teddy bear, but the original dog is still hidden somewhere in
my parents' attic. Getting our facial expressions right was fun, but also challeng-
ing. We made a blow-up of the original picture and set up a big mirror, but it took
lots of tries because one of us would break down laughing every time we tried to recapture those ridiculous expressions. Once we finally got it perfect, we framed both
pictures side by side and gave them to our mother for her sixtieth birthday.

113

A Clean Sweep

Rachel was always my little household helper. Even when she was so little that the broom was a good two feet taller than she was, she loved to swing and sweep while holding it down low, and she took her duties very seriously. Once she had swept that bad dirt out of the house, she was ready to take on the outside world. She'd often take her broom outside the clean the sidewalk with the same gusto!

— *Nancy Wagner Smith*

Guitar Hero

For months back in 1963, I had been eyeing a Martin D21 guitar that was displayed in a local music store's window. But by the time I finally had the money to buy it, it was gone. A folk group touring through my small central Canadian city of Regina had bought it. Luckily, the store had other guitars. I was taken down to the basement storeroom and allowed to play every guitar. The one with the best tone was a 1957 Martin D18, so I bought it. Anyone who ever played that instrument commented on how great it sounded.

Unfortunately, it was stolen in 1993, but, I found the excellent replacement you see in the *Now Me* picture—a limited-edition Martin D18 Vintage built to the same specs as models that were built in 1935.

— *Don Leman*

The Amazing *Spider-roos*

I was just about four years old when the Easter Bunny brought me a pair of Spider-man Underoos. Of course, when we went to Grandma and Grandpa's house for Easter breakfast later that morning, I just had to wear them. The fact that Underoos are underwear and are inappropriate for Easter attire didn't stop me from proudly showing them off. My father was so amused by the whole situation, he took a picture of me acting like a super-hero atop the family station wagon. He felt the photo needed to include a damsel in distress, too, so my little sister Marianne, appropriately attired in her Easter dress, was cast for the part.

—*Jason Gill*

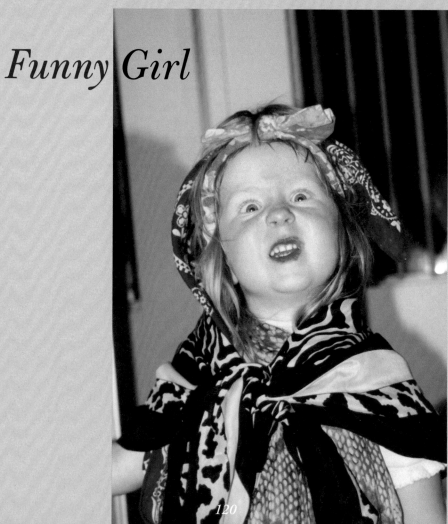

Funny Girl

I have always been able to make crazy faces like this. It must be something that runs in my family, because my brother and dad can make a lot of the same silly faces I can. I remember in seventh grade, I would make faces at my teacher, and instead of sending me to detention, she would just start laughing so hard, and class would be disrupted. It was awesome. For her Christmas present that year, I gave her a flip book of my many faces, titled "The Many Faces of Erin Leonard." When I saw her recently, she told me she still has that book after all these years!

—*Erin Leonard*

Dazed and Confused

In the *Young Me* picture, I'm at the window in my house in Springfield, Ohio, where I was born. I was only one or two, so I don't remember what I was looking at—possibly my next-door neighbor, who would often play with me, even though she was a lot older than I

was. My expression looks to me like a combination of curiosity, surprise, and agitation at being told to turn toward the camera. In the *Now Me* photo, I tried to re-create the exact same expression, even though I don't know the emotions that must have inspired it.

— *Elizabeth Kalbers*

Short End of the Shtick

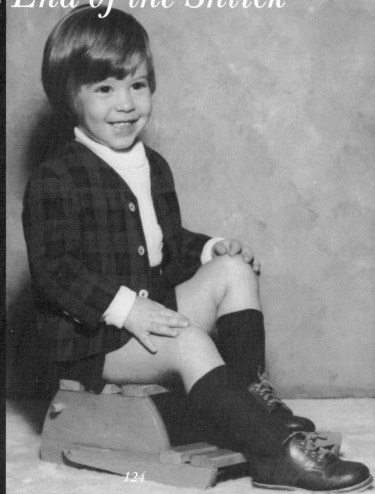

I re-created this picture as a gift to my mother on her sixty-third birthday. Duplicating the outfit was not easy. I didn't have much say about my clothing when I was a small child, but needless to say, my usual adult outfits are not in this style! I scoured local thrift shops until I found the perfect turtleneck-blazer combo to match the tastefully appointed outfit I wore as a two year old. Then my wife's shorts and cut-up blue stockings were the perfect complement. Just as I had hoped, my mom loved the diptych I gave her! It now hangs in a prominent spot in my parents' home for all their friends to see.

— *Pete Malone*

125

Smile for the Camera!

My cousin and I were enjoying our delicious popsicles. After all, orange was, and still is, our favorite flavor. But then someone wanted to take a picture of us. We agreed, but I hated having my picture taken! I never liked having to sit still, and one of the hardest things for me to do was smile on command. So that explains my facial expression of resentment and frustration. It was all over my face. My cousin didn't mind sitting for a photo the way I did, and actually, that hasn't changed for either of us.

— Elena Lazzaretto

Sands of Time

The *Young Me* picture was taken in 1985 when I was three years old. It was one of the first times I went into the ocean, and I was terrified! My mom took that picture just as a wave washed over my foot. It was a little wave but that big look of fear and anxiety on my baby face is real. I'm twenty-eight now, and my family has gone to that same beach by Dana Point, California, for the past twenty-five summers. When I thought about re-creating a photo, there was no other choice for me. I have so many memories attached to that stretch of sand that there is no place I would rather be pictured.

— *Shaun Keating*

Once a Cheesehead!
Always a Cheesehead!

Photo courtesy of Jim Ebert

Back in 1997, Mary Lynn made paper cheeseheads for her family to wear during Super Bowl XXXI in support of Wisconsin's beloved Green Bay Packers. The cheeseheads worked their magic that day as the Packers beat the New England Patriots 35 to 21. In 2011, the Packers made their first trip back to the Super Bowl in fourteen years, where they faced the Pittsburgh Steelers. With the entire Ebert family—Jim, Mary Lynn, and boys Mitch, John, and Brad—gathered again on that Super Bowl XLV Sunday, Mary Lynn made brand-new bright-yellow cheeseheads. Not only were they perfect for re-creating the original photo, they once again worked their magic as the Packers went on to beat the Steelers 31 to 25.

Race Against Time

While the item that stands out in these two pictures is my cherished baseball cap, the surprising thing about the *Young Me* photo is how special that new watch I'm holding was. It was my first one, and I had spent a lot of time whining about getting one because I was convinced I needed it since I was getting awfully grown up. There was one night a while before that picture was taken when I came home for dinner very late. Everyone was eating, and nobody said a word, but there wasn't any food in the kitchen for me. I ran upstairs and cried. Eventually my mom came to get me, and I remember telling her, "If I had a watch, this wouldn't have happened!"

— *Jim Darling*

Beauty Parlor

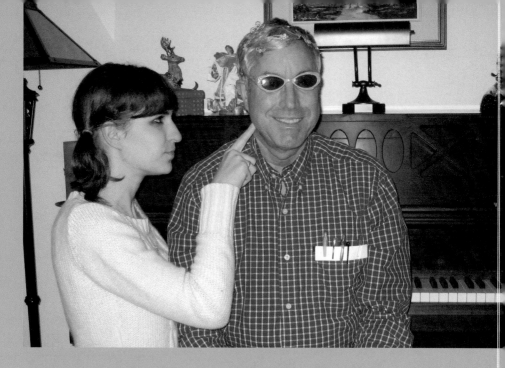

When I was a little girl, back in the mid-1980s, I loved doing my dad's hair. I'm not saying that I was good at it, and honestly, I'm not exactly a hair stylist nowadays either. I'm a shower-and-run-out-of-the-house-with-wet-hair kind of gal. But I did like making him look as goofy as I could. My dad was always a good sport about it, and thanks to his play-along attitude, we were able to laugh and smile at him together. As you can see in the *Now Me* photo, he is still a good sport about silly fun today! I only wish we still had those *classy* red sunglasses.

— *Erin Hendrickson*

No Use Crying over Spilled Popcorn

I was a cute little girl, but life is hard sometimes. Even for cute little kids. Spilling popcorn, for example, can seem fairly tragic to a small person, so what else could I do but lie there and cry? The question in my mind is, why did my parents feel this was a great time to take a picture of me? If this had been the only time they photographed me in tears, I could overlook it, but it wasn't. From what I can tell, my parents must have thought I was at my cutest when I was crying, because almost all of my childhood photos show me with tears rolling down my face.

—*Mikelle Williams*

Scootering Along

The *Young Me* picture was taken to immortalize my first day of kindergarten. Later that morning, my mom came to school with me and made a Super 8 movie that captured me walking around the classroom. The film also shows one of my new classmates, Katy, quietly sitting at a table, ready to learn. Twenty years later, the old scooter isn't looking so good, but Katy couldn't be better. She helped me take this *Now Me* photo shortly after our first wedding anniversary. At our rehearsal dinner last year, we showed my mom's home movie of the first day we met in kindergarten. It was a big hit with all our friends.

—*Dean Boshart*

Too Cool for School

I am always amazed when I look back at how cool my best friend, Zach, and I thought we were as teenagers—so cool we couldn't even look at the camera in this picture! We spent the majority of our time driving around, listening to music, and recording ourselves singing along to Beastie Boys, Violent Femmes, and Radiohead. We even had a terrifying fascination with Queen. Our favorite sing-along was always "Bohemian Rhapsody." We sang our hearts out to it, just the way Freddie Mercury did. Now, as an adult, when I start to take myself too seriously, I dig out that old micro-cassette and listen to it. We were just terrible!

—*Adam Brandt*

Fit for a King

The *Young Me* photo was taken during our celebration of the French holiday Fête des Rois, or Three Kings Day. Part of the tradition is to eat the cake called Galette des Rois. It has a dried *fève* (broad bean) hidden inside it, and whoever finds the bean becomes "King for the Day." It is a thrill to find it, but you do risk losing a tooth if you chomp down on the bean too hard. Part of your royal reward includes wearing a hideous crown like the one I have on. Back then, it didn't seem strange to me that I would win every time, so that explains my big, naïve smile. Of course, now I know that my parents cheated to let me win—I think partly because they liked seeing me wearing the silly jeweled crown.

— *Frederic Grelet*

A Kiss That
Can't Be Missed

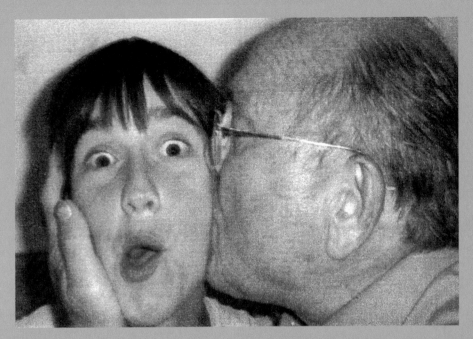

My grandfather has always been very affectionate with his family, especially us grandkids. He is the grandpa who would pinch your cheeks and give you big smooches. I've been fortunate enough to have this constant affection and attention my whole life. In the thirty years between these two pictures, he hasn't changed one bit. He will always be a sweet, caring, and thoughtful grandfather with a one-of-a-kind sense of humor. Every day I feel so lucky to have him in my life, and to have pictures like these showing his love for me.

— *Annie Strupeck*

The Big Picture

School picture day was always a big event. The *Young Me* photo is my kinder-garten picture, and I was so happy and excited to have it taken. I remember I was told not to touch my hair before it was my turn in front of the camera—they didn't want us to have tousled hair. You can see how perfect it was. But the most difficult part of the process was not being allowed to move. For a girl that age, it was hard to sit still and smile for the camera. For the *Now Me* photo, the most dif-ficult part was probably giving my hair that same perfect, not tousled look.

—*Jana Moravcová*

Circle *of Love*

Recently, as my family was looking through some keepsakes and mementos, we discovered this *Young Me* photo of my dad, me, and my two sisters. My mother took it eighteen years ago on the day my dad brought home this huge tire to make a sandbox.

After reminiscing for a while, we decided it would be fun to relive the memory by reproducing the picture. Many times in life, the simplest things bring the most comfort and closure to those who have lost a loved one, and our family had lost our mother that past year to a cancer she'd fought with strength and determination for five years. This *Now Me* photo reminds me that while she may not be in any more pictures with us, she will always be in our hearts.

— Tim Vandegrift

Photo Credits

YMNM
No. 1

—*Ze Frank*